Fee Fie Fo...
MOM!

Contents

Chapter 1 – Terrible Twins	2
Chapter 2 – Meet the Cast	9
Chapter 3 – The Big Hairy Giant	16
Chapter 4 – Two Heads Are Better Than One	22
Chapter 5 – Teamwork	28

Sîan Lewis

Illustrated by Garry Parsons

HOUGHTON MIFFLIN HARCOURT
Supplemental Publishers

www.SteckVaughn.com
800-531-5015

Chapter 1 – Terrible Twins

Sam and Samantha were twins.
They looked alike.
They sounded alike.
They were always arguing.

One Saturday morning, Mom was making breakfast.

It was a sunny day. The birds were singing. The bees were humming. Dad was whistling an out-of-tune tune.

"Breakfast!" called Mom.

From upstairs came a bang, a screech, and a yell. The birds flew away in fear. The bees stopped humming. Dad put his fingers in his ears.

"Oh, no," sighed Mom. "Those two are trying to race each other again."

The twins ran along the hall and tried to squeeze through the door.

"Get out of my way!" shrieked Samantha.
"Stop pushing me!" yelled Sam.
"Ouch!" They both crashed into the kitchen table.

SLOP! went the milk.

PITTER PATTER! went the cereal.

CLANG! went the spoons.

Sam grabbed the egg in the blue eggcup.

"Careful!" cried Mom, diving to catch the plate just in time.

"Sam took the blue eggcup!" yelled Samantha. "It's mine!"

"It's not!" yelled Sam.

Smash! went the egg.

Smash!

"Stop it!" roared Mom. "It's not funny." She picked up the phone and dialed a number. "Hello," she said. "Is this the Youth Center?"

"Yes," said a voice. "Darren speaking. How can I . . . ?" Darren held the phone away from his ear and gasped at the noise.

"Hello! Do you have any classes for nine-year-olds on Saturday mornings?" shouted Mom loudly.

"There's a drama class starting in ten minutes," Darren shouted back.

"Thank you," said Mom. "I'll bring over Sam and Samantha."

Mom put the phone down, picked up a piece of paper, and wrote:

You two are going to drama class.

Now!

Then she waved the paper in front of her noisy twins and shooed them out to the car.

Chapter 2 – Meet the Cast

Mom stopped outside the Youth Center. "Ooh, look at that poster!" she said. "The Young Drama Group is putting on a *Jack and the Beanstalk* show."

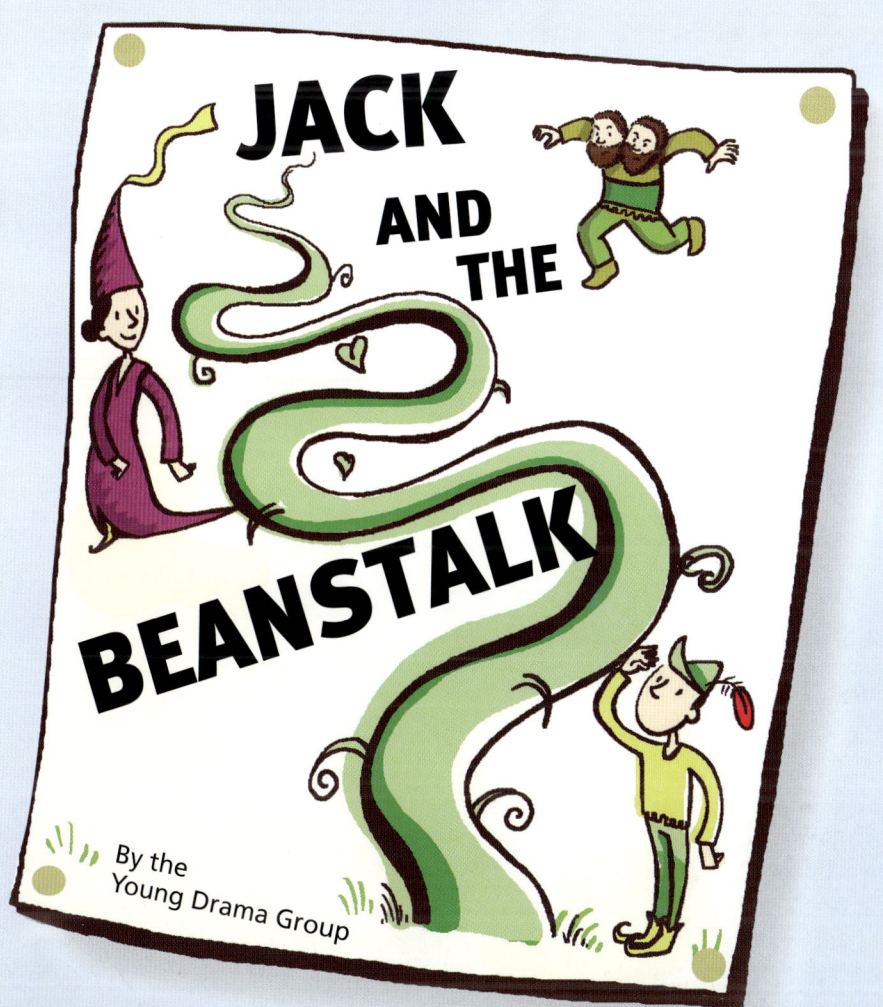

"Isn't that exciting?" said Mom.

"No," said Sam.

"It might be," said Samantha. "I wouldn't mind being that princess on the poster."

"In your dreams!" growled Sam.

"Now don't argue," said Mom. "Just stay away from each other."

"That's fine with me," said Samantha, frowning at her brother.

Just then a friendly young man put his head around the door. He smiled at the twins.

"Hi, you must be Sam and Samantha. And you're twins! That's great!" he called. "I'm Darren, the teacher. Come and meet the team."

"Hello, Darren," said Samantha, in the sort of voice a princess might use.

She ducked under his arm and stepped into the hall, where a harp plink-plonked.

"That's Katy, who plays the harp—and *plays* the harp!" said Darren.

Samantha looked. Katy wasn't just *playing* a harp. She was dressed like a harp, too.

"Hello-o," sang Katy.

"Hello!" called the other kids in the drama group.

Sam and Samantha's heads looked around the room. The place was a beehive of activity. There were people painting scenery, people making costumes, and people setting up lights. Everybody had something to do, not just the actors.

Katy wasn't the only one who was wearing a costume. Brad was waddling around dressed as a goose. Ellie was having an huge apron pinned up so she didn't trip on it, while Josh was wearing a green shirt over his jeans and pretending to fight himself in the mirror.

But who was wearing the princess dress?
No one!
The princess dress was lying on the stage on top of a hairy old rug. Samantha grinned to herself.

Chapter 3 – The Big Hairy Giant

Brad the Goose waddled up to Samantha with two sheets of paper in his beak.

"Honk! Honk! Here's a bit of the script for you to try out," he said.

"Thank you," said Samantha.

Scene Six
In the Giant's Castle

Giant: Fee Fie Fo Fum!
I smell a nasty smell.
How come?

Harp: It's Jack!

Goose: He's taken my golden egg!

Harp: And I think he's taken Princess Meg!

Giant: He won't get far.
I'll squash him flat.
And then I'll feed him to the cat.

Samantha read the first page very carefully. Then she read the second page. On both pages there were parts for the Goose, the Harp, and the Giant but none at all for Princess Meg. The Harp was Katy and the Goose was Brad. That left . . .

"Uh-oh!" whispered Samantha. Her grin disappeared. She looked across the room at Sam. Sam was reading the same two pages of the script. "Uh-oh," whispered Samantha again as an awful thought crossed her mind. Her face began to wobble, and her tummy began to feel a little strange.

"OK?" called Darren. "Ready to try out your part? I expect you've guessed by now that we're doing the story of *Jack and the Beanstalk*. We've written the words ourselves, but we can change them as we go along."

Samantha said nothing. She was watching Aisha put on the princess dress. That made her tummy feel worse.

Then Aisha reached for the hairy old rug.
"Do you want to try this on?" she called.
Samantha's eyes widened. The rug wasn't really a rug at all. It was a large giant's costume with hairy arms and a baggy old coat that reached down to the floor.
"Yes, come on," said Darren. He shooed Sam and Samantha forward and helped Aisha pull the hairy old costume over their heads.

Chapter 4 – Two Heads Are Better Than One

Sam's head popped out of the top of the Giant's costume. Samantha's head popped up beside his.

"Yuck!" gasped Sam. "What are you doing here?"

"Yuck yourself," said Samantha.

BUMP! went their noses.

"Get out of my costume!" shouted Sam.

"It's my costume, too," said Samantha.

"Don't be silly," snapped Sam. "We can't both be the Giant at the same time."

"Yes, we can," said Samantha, pointing at the mirror.

Sam nearly jumped out of his hairy skin. In the mirror a monster with two heads was staring at him.

"A two-headed giant!" he gasped. "No way! I don't want to be stuck with you."

Alarmed, Sam tried to pull the costume over his head.

"Stop it! You're pulling me, too!" yelled Samantha. She tripped over Sam's feet, and they both fell against Katy's chair.

"Eeeeek!" cried Katy, and before the Giant could stop her, her chair went whizzing across the room.

> Honk! Honk! Hooray!

The Giant's two faces turned bright red.

"Sorry, Katy!" they both cried. "We're very, very sorry!"

"You don't have to be!" said Katy, whizzing back. She was grinning from ear to ear. "That was really funny."

"Really, really funny," said Josh.

"Three cheers for our giant. Honk! Honk! Hooray!" said the Goose.

"We never thought of having a giant with two *fighting* heads before," said Aisha excitedly.

"Let's add some fighting parts to our play," said Katy.

"Yes!" said the rest of the team.

Katy fished out a pen and a sheet of paper from the side of her chair. Sam and Samantha watched as everyone gathered around her to change the script.

BUMP!

"Hey, come on you two," Josh called to them.

"You are going to join in, aren't you?" said Ellie.

The two heads of the Giant turned to each other.

"Are you?" growled one.

"Try and stop me!" grinned the other.

BUMP! went their noses.

Chapter 5 – Teamwork

Back at home, Sam and Samantha's mom and dad had enjoyed a quiet morning. Now it was time to pick up the twins.

Mom parked behind the Youth Center. The back door was open, and she could hear the children acting. She listened.

"Fee Fie Fo Fum! Let's catch Jack!"

THUMP!

BANG!

CRASH!

"Sounds exciting!" thought Mom. Then her face turned pale.

"Let's go this way!" yelled a voice she knew.

"No, this way!" yelled another.

"Stop pulling!"

"Stop pushing!"

"Take your horrible nose out of my ear."

"Ouch! You're hurting me."

"Oh, no!" gasped Mom. She rushed through the back door and ran up the stairs.

"Sam! Samantha! Please stop fighting!" Mom yelled. "It's not funny!"

"Fee Fie Fo . . . MOM!" gasped the Giant as an angry Mom ran onto the stage.

The stage went silent.

Mom turned around and nearly jumped out of her skin. There behind her stood a hairy monster.

The monster had two heads. One was Sam's, and the other was Samantha's. Both heads were looking at her very, very seriously.

"Fee Fie Fo Fum," growled the head on the right.

"What shall we do with the noisy one?" said the head on the left.

"Oops!" said Mom. "I'm sorry. I thought you were arguing."

"Us?" said Sam and Samantha. "We never argue. We're a team!"

"Yes, they're a team within our team," laughed Darren, "and they are very, very funny!"